WHAT'S IT LIKE TO BE A...?

FASHION DESIGNER

Elizabeth Dowen   Lisa Thompson

Reprinted 2009
First published in the UK 2008 by
A & C Black Publishing Ltd
36 Soho Square
London
W1D 3QY
www.acblack.com

Copyright © 2008 Blake Publishing
Published 2007 by Black Education Pty Ltd, Australia

ISBN: 978-1-4081-0511-5

Written by Lisa Thompson and Elizabeth Dowen
Publisher: Katy Pike
Series Editor: Eve Tonelli
Cover Design: Terry Woodley
Designer: Matt Lin
Printed in China by South China Printing Co. Ltd.

Cover image © Jim Arbogast/Photodisc Red

Illustration credits: p7 (br)–Mattel; p23 (br)–
Stuart Weitzman, New York; p31 (tr)–sass&bide; p4 (bl), p9(middle), p15
(bl), p15 (middle), p19 (bl), p20 (br), p26 (tr), p27 (br)–Shutterstock

This book is produced using paper made from wood grown in managed,
sustainable forests. It is natural, renewable and recyclable. The logging and
manufacturing processes conform to the environmental regulations of the
country of origin.

All the Internet addresses given in this book were correct at the time of
going to press. The author and publishers regret any inconvenience caused
if addresses have changed or sites have ceased to exist, but can accept no
responsibility for any such changes.

Contents

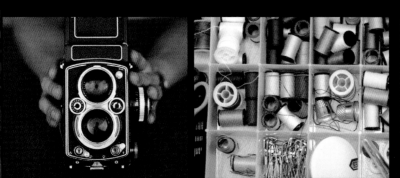

Fashion week invitation

Although there are over 100,000 people employed in the UK in the clothing and fashion industry, only a tiny fraction of those actually work as designers! You have to be determined and dedicated to get into the industry as a designer, and take every opportunity to gain work experience.

Wow! Talk about all my dreams coming true! I'm IN! I've just received an email confirming my place at Fashion Week.

To: Chloe Leong, fashion designer@Hype
Subject: Fashion Week
Sent: January 6th

Dear Chloe,
We are pleased to offer you a show at this year's Fashion Week.

Your show will be on April 13th in the 7pm timeslot. You will be required to s

It's time to think rock star style!

hype

ang
a c
st ent

So much to do! My mind is spinning with ideas. Maybe I'll do 1970s hippie inspired clothes, or ... how about a military theme? No, I think I'll go for rock star style! That's perfect for Hype — because we're a street label for guys and girls.

The hippy style might be good ...

Perhaps an army theme?

Rock star style? Yes, that's it!

I want the tops to have attitude, and the trousers to be easy to wear yet stylish. The clothes should feel loose and casual — but look cool.

I think I'll use lots of racer red and jet black for that rocker look, and do T-shirts with funky stencilling and prints, like that one I spotted in a shop in New York's SoHo area on my last trip there.

I have to start sketching right now!

Then there is the fashion show to organise. I will need a theme for the show. Who can I hire to produce it? I'll also need a stylist, and hair and make-up artists. And what about the music?

I need to write a big list of things to do — and call my team together. It's action stations!

SoHo

I want my fashion show to be professional yet exciting.

To Do:

hype

Action stations!

Property of Chloe Leong — creator and fashion designer of

>hype
the coolest street label

To do list

- research current fashion trends
- collect images of rock star style
- come up with lots of ideas
- decide which ideas work best
- choose colour schemes
- start sketching designs
- organise my team
- choose who to work on our show

There's no time to lose!

All this has to be done — in four months!

some rock star style research images

>hype

Which colours will work best?

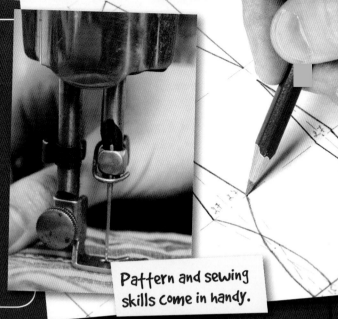

Designing clothes is only one part of running a fashion label. As well as designing, you need to know how to make the clothes and sell them. It helps if you have good skills in pattern making and sewing. That way you can make your ideas become a reality yourself!

Pattern and sewing skills come in handy.

That's often how fashion designers start doing everything themselves; the designing and pattern making, then sewing and selling their clothes. That's okay if you are doing a few pieces and small ranges. I used to do it all myself too, but now my business is too big for one person to manage.

Sometimes, you're the one making the sale too!

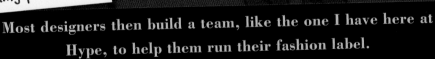

Most designers then build a team, like the one I have here at Hype, to help them run their fashion label.

DIDYOUKNOW?

CHILD'S PLAY IS BIG BUSINESS

Fashion designers in the 1500s displayed their designs by crafting doll-sized versions of their fashions and taking them to shows.

They may make small clothes, but one of the leading producers of clothing is the Mattel company — who make the clothes for their Barbie dolls!

Here's Barbie in one of her latest outfits.

7

Meet the **)hype team**

Designer / creative director

I come up with the ideas and designs for the label. I sketch the designs, decide on the number and type of garments (pieces of clothing) and choose the fabric and trims.

I'm in charge of the look of Hype and create the style of our clothes. It is my job to be aware of trends and to give the label an original direction.

hard at work

Love this image — maybe for a T-shirt?

What do you think of these designs?

Pattern makers

Eva and Ben make the patterns from my design sketches. They make different sizes of each pattern (this is called grading) so the design is ready to be made.

Eva—the pattern genius

These guys turn my sketches into patterns.

S   M   Lg

We need all sizes for our collection.

8

Sample maker / machinist

Julianna is a whiz on the sewing machine. She sews together the prototype (sample) of a new design with fabric cut from the pattern that Eva or Ben has created. Julianna also gives us production information, such as how long a garment will take to make, the best way to make it and the costs involved.

Julianna creating a new sample

Julianna works out the time and money we need to make these clothes too.

So many ideas for my rock theme ... What to do?

Sample models

Viv and Liam are our contract models. They come in when we need them to try on sample clothes, so we can see what works and what needs to be changed. This is very important. Sometimes you can have an idea that looks good on paper but when you put it on a real person, it looks awful.

Liam is our male model.

Viv loves modelling my new designs.

Meet the >hype team

Production manager

Once we are happy with the garments, Jason plans the making (production) of them. There are lots of things to organise to make sure things run as smoothly as possible.

Fabric is ordered and collected from wholesalers and textile mills. Sometimes fabric needs to be printed, dyed or embroidered before it is cut. This is also Jason's job to organise.

Jason makes sure all the deliveries come in on time and the quality standards of our clothes are met. It's a big job — you have to be very organised!

Jason coordinates all parts of the production process.

a textile mill

Everything has to be kept on track.

on-time delivery

Too pretty for rock? Could be a good contrast.

I want attitude for my range!

Business manager / creative director

Robert manages Hype's finances. He makes sure we have money to run the company, and pay our staff and suppliers.

Robert also helps me look after our buyers. He is always looking for new clients and places to promote and sell Hype. Robert advertises what Hype is all about to get our buyers and the press interested and excited about what we're creating.

Robert looks after the money.

on the promotion trail

We use professional photographs to showcase our collection.

We need the press to publicise our clothes.

Banded Together...

Not rock enough – too country and western!

Where's it made?

Most clothing is made outside a company's headquarters.

The patterns and the fabric are sent to the cutters, who cut out the fabric pieces. These pieces then go to the machinists, along with all the different trims like zips, buttons, thread — everything they will need to make the clothing.

When different parts of a process are done in different locations like this, it's called outsourcing.

outsourcing

MADE IN CHINA
FABRIQUE EN CHINE

11

How I became a fashion designer

The first person who taught me about fashion design was my mum. She would make new outfits for me and my sister every weekend. Some were very, very strange!

I think the sunglasses make the outfit!

I've always loved clothes and dressing up. Even when I was younger, I was forever putting different outfits together. I made sure I had the right shoes, jewellery and bag to go with any outfit.

How does it look?

Lots of kids in my neighbourhood liked dressing up.

In secondary school, I studied textile design and art, and I would sketch and make outfits for me and my friends. After school, I wanted to learn more about fashion, so I enrolled on an Art and Design Foundation Diploma course, which led on to a Fashion Design Higher National Diploma (HND) at college.

Mum giving me some fashion tips!

Selling in markets is a great way to start.

During our final year at college, I began selling my designs at a local market. When I finished my HND, I carried on selling my clothes there and even convinced some shops in the area to stock my designs too.

Getting my clothes into local shops was a real breakthrough.

One day, a buyer for a chain of street wear stores saw my clothes at the market. He asked if I would be able to make clothes for his shops and gave me his card.

When I called him the next day and he told me how many clothes he wanted, I nearly fell over. It was five times more than I was used to producing. I quickly realised that to fill the order I would need financial help.

name (prin

signatu

I needed money to get started in the big time.

My idea, and the real thing!

A family friend decided to invest in my business and Hype was born. It is often stressful and always a lot of work, but seeing someone walking down the street in one of my designs is a huge buzz and makes all the effort worthwhile.

FASHION
STEP-BY-STEP

The steps in producing a garment

STEP 1 — think of styles, get inspired

STEP 2 — sketch designs

STEP 3 — research styles and ideas

STEP 4 — choose fabrics and trim

STEP 5 — finalise designs

STEP 6 — make patterns

STEP 7 — create sample range and style book

STEP 8 — sampling and fitting cycle

STEP 9 — show range to buyers

STEP 10 — buyers place orders

STEP 11

full-scale production begins

- check and grade patterns
- receive and check fabrics
- spread fabrics and cut garments
- bundle cut garments into sizes and styles
- send cut work to machinists
- finish garments — buttons and buttonholes
- cleaning and pressing
- quality control
- tagging and packing

STEP 12 — send to retailers

STEP 13 — garments checked and priced

£19.99

STEP 14 — retail displays created

STEP 15 — the consumer (you) buys them

SOLD

DIDYOUKNOW?

LEFT AND RIGHT

Women's shirt buttons fasten up on the left because when buttons were first used during the Victorian period, ladies were dressed by their maids. The buttons were put on the servants' right side – the women's left, to make it easier for them to be buttoned up.

15

A good fashion designer needs

- passion and flair for fashion
- creative flair for colour, style, texture and shape
- understanding of how to use fabrics
- knowledge of production procedures
- an eye for detail
- sketching and ICT skills
- technical skills like garment construction and pattern making
- ability to identify and develop trends
- problem solving skills
- sound business sense
- great people and team working skills
- competitive nature
- belief in yourself and your work
- ability to work under pressure and meet deadlines

About the Fashion and Clothing Industry...

Haute couture is the area of fashion where people can pay thousands of pounds for an individually-made, original garment. Designers often work with individual customers, linking their designs to occasions on which the outfits will be worn.

Wholesale couture/ designer-label garments are made and sold to retail shops. Relatively few of each garment are produced. Designers may follow trends set by the haute couture designers, or create their own styles. Many British designers have become successful in this field.

Craft and small businesses may have just one designer and a small support team. The designer organises production, and may also be involved in marketing and administration.

Wholesale manufacturers or *mass production companies* supply retail chains and mail-order firms, as well as marketing their own brand names. The designer often works within a design team, and may also be part of a management team with buyers, costing experts, merchandisers and production staff.

A college course really helped me.

Most people become designers by studying design at college, where they learn about the technical and artistic areas of the subject.

After college, many designers begin their careers working as design assistants in fashion houses. Fashion assistants normally work in the fashion room alongside the pattern cutters, sample machinists and other designers.

a fashion house

Very few designers have had no formal fashion training, and just start making and selling clothes.

Fashion design is a very competitive area. Having a qualification does not guarantee you a job! Courses that include work experience provide a chance for you to create a good portfolio – always of interest to prospective employers.

It takes a lot of determination and skill to get your clothes hanging in the shops.

Events like Graduate Fashion Week are an important opportunity for a small number of new graduates to showcase their talent.

FACT FILE: WHAT'S INVOLVED?

Fashion design is a production-focused job that involves meetings, deadlines, budgeting, negotiating with suppliers and long hours.

INITIAL INSPIRATION

I always carry a journal everywhere I go. That way, if I get a flash of inspiration, I can just jot it down. My journals are full of ideas, scribbles, pictures, photos, invitations and clippings — anything that catches my eye.

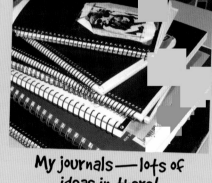

My journals — lots of ideas in there!

Take a peek inside.

I keep most of my research in my journals too. I look out for new colours, fabrics, trims and accessories. This is called trend forecasting.

my inspiration boards

FACT FILE: CREATIVE METHODS

Designers have different ways of working. Some sketch their ideas on paper, while others work directly with the fabric itself, draping and folding it until they find the right shape — or they adapt patterns from previous collections. In small firms, they may then do their own pattern cutting, but in larger organisations they work with a team of pattern cutters and machinists, and with production managers.

You can sketch ... or work directly onto a mannequin.

Plan ahead.

Things that need to be considered when designing a garment:
1) Who is the garment for?
2) When will it be worn (which season)?
3) What is the cost of producing the garment?

Designers also visit trade fairs and shows – in this country and abroad – to find out about new designs, fabrics and products.

HIGH TECH STYLE GURUS

These days, I, like many designers, get a lot of my information and inspiration from Internet trend services. These companies, like the Worth Global Style Network (www.wgsn.com), provide up-to-the-minute information on the latest popular styles from around the world. News, research and photographs show everything from catwalk shows in Milan and celebrities in Rio, to what people are wearing on the streets of Amsterdam.

The world is at your fingertips.

TECHNOLO HIGHLIG

Technology helps you find out who's wearing what and where!

The internet is a way for modern style industries, including fashion, cosmetics and interior design, to keep their finger on the pulse of what's new, hip and happening — without having to travel to many different countries each year, which takes time and money.

THE DRAWING BOARD

Sometimes I draw my designs by hand, at other times I use my computer — using design programs like Photoshop or Illustrator — so I can easily change the colour or fabric of a design to see what it would look like.

some idea doodles

A lot of my designs start off like these rough sketches.

Your computer is your best friend. Know how to use it.

Ta-da— the real thing!

FACT FILE: TYPES OF FASHION

Nearly all fashion items fit into one of three types — the fad, the standard and the classic.

The fad
This is the latest craze. The fad garment generally lasts one or two seasons. Remember fluffy leg warmers and neon tights?

Check out those leg warmers!

So, what's in this season?

FACT FILE: THE HOUSE OF WORTH

Charles Frederick Worth (1826–1895) is regarded as the first fashion designer. Before he set up his fashion house in Paris, clothing design and creation was done by seamstresses and high fashion was influenced by styles worn in the royal courts.

1823 ball gown

1883 Paris fashion

Breaking with the tradition of customers dictating the design, Charles Worth asked customers to choose from his own designs, which he displayed on models at shows.

Due to his success, customers would attach a label of his name to his designs to show they were from the House of Worth. This started the tradition of designers being not only the creative heads of fashion houses but the symbols of brands as well.

The standard
These items are the look of the season. These dresses, shirts and pants will reflect the current season's style, cut, colour and fabric.

The classic
This constant, functional and versatile item never goes out of style — like the little black dress, the blazer or the trench coat.

a little black dress

looking good in a blazer

FASHION THEMES

Each fashion range has an overall theme. Designing around themes gives me a focus. Themes might be inspired by a place in the world, a specific subculture or even a movie.

the Moulin Rouge in Paris

cowboy-inspired fashion

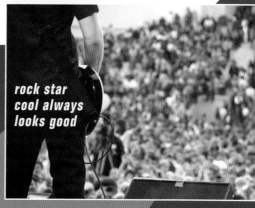
rock star cool always looks good

Themes allow the garments to have a similar feel and look. That way, all the fabrics and colours that make up the range look like they belong together.

There are different categories of clothes within each themed range. Categories group garments around their functions (like sportswear or casual). For these categories, I don't just design the clothes. I design the total look including bags, hats or jewellery – in fact, any accessories I can think of to go with the clothes.

the accessories needed for a chic style

accessories for a bohemian look

The categories for my rock star themed range are:

On the street — clothes for chilling out
• cargo trousers and T-shirts, casual but cool

after dark style

on the street style

Free style — sporty/functional clothes
• tracksuits and vest tops, combining comfort with looking good

After dark — clothes for going out
• funky shirts and tops, bold trousers, skirts and dresses, really out there!

I did some research and sketching on rock star style during my last holiday in New York. I try to go on inspirational trips to different fashion capitals around the world — London, New York, Tokyo, Paris or Milan. Seeing what's happening out there helps get my creative juices flowing!

Greetings from London

Welcome to New York

Bellissimo Milano

Every city has a different take on fashion. Paris and Milan are about classic style and elegance — whereas New York, London and Tokyo are more about taking fashion risks and creating bold, new designs.

Tokyo has a confident take on fashion.

DIDYOUKNOW?

There's no shoes quite like these

The most expensive shoes in the world were ruby slippers, inspired by the pair worn by Judy Garland in the movie, *The Wizard of Oz*. Made by American shoe designer Stuart Weitzman, they were worth around $2.3 million and had a full-time security guard to watch over the 642 rubies in them.

That's a lot of rubies!

23

COLOUR, TEXTURE AND PATTERN

Colour

Colour is a Hype trademark. I use unusual colour combinations like:
- pink/orange
- blue/green
- purple/ lime

I keep a colour wheel picture on my desk for reference.

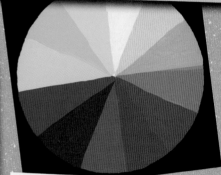

Every designer needs a colour wheel.

For unique colours, our fabrics are dyed beforehand. I work out the fabrics, colours and trims that we will use, and then I create storyboards so everyone knows what goes with what.

tie-dying in action

Trim includes anything other than fabric that we add onto garments – zips, buttons, ties and beads.

My storyboards have all the information we need to create the clothes.

Beads, anyone?

Colour, colour and more colour

In fashion lingo, colours fall into four main groups:

1. Staple colours
Colours that are used every year and are liked by all age groups in all seasons, for example, black, white, navy blue, grey.

Black and white never go out of style.

Definitely a summer colour!

2. Seasonal colours
Colours that remind us of different times of the year:
light + bright colours = summer,
warm + dark colours = winter.

Warm browns keep us snug in winter.

3. Fashion colours
Colours that dominate each fashion season and vary from year to year — one year pastels might be in, the next it could be jungle commando colours.

a camouflage-inspired hat

4. Accent colours
Small amounts of colour that contrast with the main one — like a green zip on a red jacket.

Accent colours give clothes an interesting look.

You can come up with thousands of different colour schemes with new shades by mixing existing colours.

Colour crazy

- Monochrome colours are shades of the same colour — like dark blue, mid-blue and light blue.
- Complementary colours bounce off each other. They sit on opposite sides of the colour wheel, like blue and orange.
- Harmonious colours are on either side of a main colour on the colour wheel — like yellow-orange and yellow-green on either side of yellow.

a monochrome shirt — all shades of blue

The orange and blue lanterns on this design of mine are complementary colours.

25

COLOUR, TEXTURE
AND PATTERN

Texture

Texture means the feel of something. It could be smooth, grainy or silky. Texture is important for clothes because we touch and wear them, so I need to get it just right. Fabric (cloth) plays a large part in creating texture.

Customers want clothes to last so I've got to think about that when I'm designing.

Fabric

A good knowledge of fabrics is essential for designing and making clothes. I always need to think about how clothes feel, how they sit on the body, how long they last and how they should be cared for.

Fabrics come in many types, and fabric producers are always coming up with new materials. For example, they can be knitted, woven, non-woven, bonded or felted.

Trims

Texture can be created with trims, such as patches, beads or buttons. Ribbon threaded through garments, ruffles, pleating and quilting also all affect the feel of clothes.

Getting it right

When a designer is satisfied with a design, a sample is made. This sample is made in a plain fabric, such as calico, and is called a toile. A toile can be altered and reshaped until the look is just right.

making a toile

Pattern

Pattern is another factor in fashion design. Patterns can be very seasonal — one year, animal prints are in, the next it can be spots or stripes. I love making up different patterns for fabric. Here are some of my favourites.

How about stripes?

Paisley print

You can also use swirls, polka dots, retro-style Paisley print or floral designs, to name just a few. For the new Hype ranges, I'm thinking of using stripes and tartan. We'll see!

Think I'll use tartan too.

Fabric and fibres

Fabric threads are called fibres.
Fibres can be:
- natural — cotton, linen, wool, silk;
- manufactured — nylon, polyester, micro fibre, lycra.

Some fabrics are a mix of both types.

Wool and silk are two natural fibres.

Lycra and nylon are synthetic fibres.

27

hYpe

The Business of Fashion

A designer hard at work!

$\mathcal{D}$esigners work at least six months ahead of each season. That means I'm designing swimwear in the middle of winter and big, woolly jackets when all I can think about is going to the beach! So I have to be very focused.

This dress made the final cut.

$\mathcal{B}$ig fashion houses can produce up to four ranges per year, with an average of 70 garments per range. Many more garments are made but most will be discarded, as only the very best will make it onto the catwalk.

It's going to be a rocking summer!

$\mathcal{H}$ere at Hype, we have two ranges per year — our winter and summer ranges. For Fashion Week, I'm creating a summer range. I've decided that the theme for Hype's summer range this year will be rock star style.

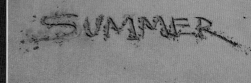

28

French for fashion

Haute couture is French for high dressmaking. This is where people pay thousands of pounds for made-to-order, original garments. Designers often work with individual customers, linking their designs to occasions when the outfit will be worn. They use expensive, high-quality materials and finishes.

Wow, that's a cool dress.

Most designers create ready to wear (*prêt-à-porter*) clothing ranges that are produced in various amounts and prices. Even couture houses make ready-to-wear lines to sell to the public.

Not sure about that flowery shirt!

What does a fashion buyer do?

Fashion buyers work for large shops and buy ranges of clothes to be sold in their stores. Buyers attend fashion shows all over the world to order clothes from both local and international designers.

Buyers choose which clothes end up in the shops.

A buyer must know the type of person who shops in their stores and predict the clothes they will want. They need a sharp eye to spot upcoming trends so they can buy clothes that will be in demand. Being a buyer, like being a sales manager, requires excellent communication skills and good business sense.

Those people in the audience are buyers.

hype

Organising the SHOW

Why have a fashion show?
A fashion show gives me, as a designer, an opportunity to be creative and daring, to show how I would like my clothes to be worn.

A show is also a creative marketplace for buyers from different shops. They get to see the clothes and how they can be worn. This helps them decide what they want to order. Fashion magazine editors also get to see what designers are doing and what they have created for a future season.

There are many different types of fashion shows.

Shows are very competitive. Buyers and magazine editors will only buy and review the best ranges. A great show can put your clothes in all the top magazines and make everyone want to wear them.

Fashion editors want the latest looks in their magazines.

Will this dress be chosen?

We want people to rush out to buy our clothes.

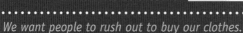

Fashion is not just about clothes, it is also about style and image. A show is a fun way to present the style and image of the label as well as this season's theme. Shows are also an exciting way of building and marketing a fashion brand.

one of our magazine pages

I have hired Alex Johns to produce the Hype Rock Star Style show. He is perfect for the job because he uses lots of colour and drama. Alex's role is to make the show happen.

Shows help label names to be instantly recognisable.

A good show producer will be bursting with ideas!

He puts together the lighting, music and staging to create the show. It is important that everything reflects the mood of the clothes. I want the show to have the energy of a rock concert!

a wedding dress

two Japanese women wearing kimonos

DIDYOUKNOW?

Why we wear what we do

Specific clothes and fashion styles may be worn for all kinds of reasons:

- a special occasion, like a wedding
- cultural tradition — a kimono in Japan or kilts in Scotland
- religious reasons — wearing a Jewish kippah (skull cap)
- practicality — Eskimos wear big coats in their frozen homeland
- to make a fashion statement — punk or gothic styles

Now, that's a fashion statement!

a Scottish piper in his kilt

Eskimos need to wrap up to keep warm!

HYPE ROCK STAR SHOW
countdown

Aargh, I can't find the perfect material!

Jan 10

I'm searching through piles of fabric samples, trying to choose which to use. It is very frustrating. We can't get enough of the one I really like, and another doesn't come in the colour I need. I wonder if there is time to dye it? I might not be able to get it delivered in time ... the search goes on.

I have the same issues with the trims. I spend lots of time asking questions like 'Can I get that zip in this colour?'; 'Do you have these toggles in that style?'; 'What sizes are available for these buttons?'; 'How many of those beads can we get in time?'

← So many beads, so little time.

I need more colours!

Designing can be such a roller-coaster ride. One minute, I am feeling great — riding high on excitement about an idea. The next minute, I am confused and deflated as I run into problems trying to turn that idea into a reality.

Jan 12

Eventually, I manage to find what I want and I am riding high again. Most designers go through this. I guess it comes with wanting things to be just right.

I'm also doing research on the Internet trend sites for inspiration for the Hype look that I need to capture on my storyboards.

I imagine the range will include ripped, tight jeans and vintage T-shirts. There'll be tartan miniskirts, accessories like looping metal wallet chains and lightning flash earrings.

SEARCH

I'm back online to do more research.

So, this is what they're wearing in Europe at the moment.

My inspiration board is full of ideas!

Can you see my theme?

33

My mannequin is waiting for clothes to wear.

I'm running out of pencils!

Jan 14

I am now well into the design process and I'm madly sketching my ideas. It's sketching, sketching and more sketching.

a more detailed colour chart helps

I love this T-shirt — very rock star!

Jan 20

Things are starting to take shape. I'm drawing up some of the storyboards for the range.

Storyboards are useful because they show how I want the clothes to look. They also have a sample of the fabrics and colours so I can get an idea of the feel of the garments as well.

pattern time already

Feb 9

Eva and Ben have begun to make patterns from my design sketches. Some fabric has already been cut so Julianna can start on the samples. This is when my ideas become reality — the exciting part!

Once Julianna has the sample garments ready, I will ask my part-time models, Viv and Liam, to come in to try them on.

← Julianna's on the sewing machine.

Feb 20

Viv and Liam model the samples. This is where we see how the garments fit the body for the first time. Are the legs too short or the sleeves too long? How about the waist? Is it too tight, too low or too high?

Well, this T-shirt looks good with a guitar on!

We also get our first look at the finish of the clothes. Are the seams neat? Should they be double or single stitched? Does the fabric hang right? Do all the outside finishes on the garment, like pockets, buttonholes and top stitching, match the style?

The small finishes make all the difference.

Liam's rock star hair style!

The first sample garments are ready.

Changes are always made. Things are taken out, off, up and apart. Sometimes I create something totally different.

Sketches like this

become style cards

Style 1:

which end up as clothes like these!

Feb 24

Now I'm finalising the designs. Each design has a style number or name. I write up cards for each design that include a sketch, trim list and samples of fabric stapled to them, so everyone can easily see what each design will look like.

Mar 2

Everything is coming along well. We are all into a design routine; sample — make changes — new sample — send to machinists. I love this bit.

Mar 6

My life is a blur of fittings, fittings, fittings.

Mar 9

Panic stations! Help!

I've lost my team! Eva and Ben are both sick. Robert is out organising press releases and media coverage for the show, whilst Julianna is sewing at half pace, distracted because she is moving house!

Fabrics have started to arrive and stores are ringing to reorder clothes from the last range. There is SO much going on!

Come on Julianna, I need you!

36

Can someone get that please??

Mar 16

My pattern gurus are well again. Julianna has got her personal life under control and everyone is back on track. Phew!

Robert finds a super stylist called Zephyr who will put together the look of the clothes for the catwalk. We have very similar ideas and I'm thrilled when he books a hairdresser called Stacey and the make-up artist Kate to do the models' hair and make-up. Perfect.

I send the fabric to the cutters where it will be cut, bundled and sent onto the machinists to add all the trimmings. There are still so many things left to prepare.

It is all systems go. This show is going to blow everyone away!

I'm using some of my favourite patterns.

Hooray, the team's back together.

Zephyr — style guru.

Kate's a genius with make-up, what a scoop to get her!

Stacey's hair salon

found the ribbons!

Meeting in Progress!

Mar 17–29
The rest of March disappears in meetings ... meetings ... meetings ...

How about the hair loose and wild?

Chloe to Stacey

I love the make-up with these strong colours — very rock star!

Chloe to Kate

Lights? How many? Where? When? Alex????!!!

Chloe talking to herself — and Alex

Music? Ahhh I think I like that one? No. Maybe more like this? (This is such a hard decision because the music is so important.) Oh, hang on. That sounds good.

Chloe to Alex

Zephyr, I'm not sure. Do you think those shoes really go with that outfit?

Chloe to Zephyr

The bags are a super touch. Will all the models need hats for that story too? What other accessories do we need?

Chloe to Zephyr

I also spend hours with my team, sorting through the hundreds of model cards that have flooded in, to pick the models for the show.

When the final models are chosen, we ask them to come in and I decide who will wear what. The clothes are slightly altered so that all the clothes fit everyone perfectly. We take polaroids so we can remember what goes on whom!

Rehearsals for the show begin and I send out the invitations.

Mar 30
Only two weeks before the show. Everyone at Hype is working VERY long hours putting everything together and getting garments and accessories ready.

This is when I start to get nervous. The big day is looming. Will they like my concept? Will they like the clothes? Will everything be finished in time??

dark = warm, light = cool

VERONICA

ALISHA

TYRONE

ALEX

WINSTON

Smile!

Right, who did we forget?

OPEN 24/7

We're all working around the clock.

DIDYOUKNOW?

FEELING HOT OR COLD?
Dark colours absorb light energy whilst light colours and white reflect light. Therefore, when light shines on your dark jacket, the fabric absorbs light energy.

The absorbed energy causes electrons in the atoms of the jacket to vibrate. This activity releases heat energy, which makes the jacket — and you — warmer. That's why we wear more dark colours in winter and more light colours in summer.

39

Apr 6

Only seven days to go — will we be ready? I keep worrying that I've forgotten something but it looks like we have everything under control. My range is almost complete, just some last minute, late night adjustments to make.

Apr 11 – Two days to go!

I rush off to my last meeting with the Fashion Week organisers. Details like our guest list and the timing of the music and lights are discussed. To my relief, it's all agreed on without a hitch. Right, now what am I going to wear??

Looks quiet now. You wait until later!

Checking the stage

Apr 13
THE DAY OF THE SHOW

The clothes are put into bundles for each of the models so everyone knows who is wearing what. They are pressed and hung on the racks along with all their accessories. That way, the models can get changed as quickly as possible each time they come off stage.

Alex and I run through a quick last-minute rehearsal with the models, testing the music and lights too. I am very nervous. The tension is high because some things are still not ready. We make changes right up to the last second. Everyone is tired but running on adrenalin with all the anticipation at the same time.

Time to put out the reserved signs.

Front of house, we are busy checking the chairs. There will be reserved seats for buyers, editors and our special guests in the front rows. We want the buyers and editors up close so they get the best view of the clothes.

40

As I rush backstage, Stacey and Kate begin to work their magic with the models' hair and make-up.

Stacey working her magic.

Doing everyone's make-up takes hours.

I'm so nervous! My stomach is full of butterflies.

This model is ready to go.

SHOW TIME!

7 pm —
Lights! Music! Models! Action! The music starts and the house lights fade as the catwalk comes alive in a blaze of colour. The models strut their stuff to the funky music. The butterflies in my stomach are replaced with excited energy as I watch from the side of the stage.

The boys get into the mood backstage.

This is it! It's happening!

The clothes look FANTASTIC!

Backstage, it's a mad rush — models changing, stylists working overtime, while clothes fly everywhere. Onstage, everything looks cool and professional, going just as planned.

On stage it looks perfect!

Backstage it's madness getting everyone ready.

Are they smiling?

Good, everyone's got the right shoes!

I duck out the side to see the faces of the audience but it's hard with all the lights swirling. I see the buyers and the fashion editors scribbling down notes. The photographers are madly snapping away. What are they thinking? Is it good or bad? I will know soon enough.

Another one of my outfits being modelled for the cameras!

There are lots of photographers here. Great!

Everything is happening so fast. It's all a blur. Suddenly, the show is over and I walk onstage with all the models surrounding me. Everyone goes wild with applause. It's my moment in the spotlight and I can't quite believe I'm here. Unreal!

Afterwards, I wander through the crowd and hear snippets of conversations.
'Just mad!'
'This Hype collection is the best yet. It's fresh and exciting …'

All the hard work has been worth it. Now it's time to celebrate!

I'm happy with the photo shoots — this is just how I imagined the clothes would look.

Over the next few weeks, orders are confirmed with agents, buyers and retailers. The range goes into production so it can be in the stores for the beginning of the season for you to buy.

in the shops now

After the show
Robert is ecstatic. His phone is ringing nonstop with buyers placing orders. We have five new overseas buyers interested in the range. Fashion editors want comments, and fashion stylists are asking for pieces to use in photo shoots.

DIDYOUKNOW?

CATWALK CRAZE

Fashion Weeks around the world are now huge events. At London Fashion Week in September 2007, there were 58 designers showing their new designs on the catwalk — including international names like Betty Jackson, Jasper Conran and Nicole Farhi.

Now it's time for me to think of a new range for the next season and start all over again!
I wonder what the next Hype range will be like?
Now, let me think …

I ♥ FASHION

FOLLOW THESE STEPS TO BECOME A FASHION DESIGNER

1. Studying GCSE subjects like art, textiles, maths and business studies at school will be useful. Build up your skills in sketching, your knowledge of textiles and design, sewing and pattern making.

Start with these subjects at school.

2.a Qualifications

You can then continue by taking AS and A2 qualifications in Art and Design. Alternatively, take the BTEC National qualifications in Art and Design specialising in fashion and clothing. This provides entry to technician-level employment or higher education.

2.b Appenticeships

Apprenticeships and Advanced Apprenticeships, leading to NVQ levels 2 and 3 respectively, offer young people a route into the clothing industry. Apprenticeships may lead to work such as pattern cutter, sample technician or garment technologist

DIDYOUKNOW?

Building a design portfolio of your work is very important to get a job as a fashion designer. People will want to see examples of your ideas and designs. Start collecting them now so you have something really special to show them!

one of my original portfolio pages

If you can, create your idea into a real piece of clothing.

– whose work includes advising on garment construction methods and overseeing fabric testing and the fitting of first samples. For more information about Apprenticeships, see the 'Can U Cut It?' website listed on page 47 or contact your local Connexions/careers service.

Working from the bottom up will provide you with great skills and experience. And then who knows where you'll end up?

3. Most designers have an HND or degree in Fashion Design. The usual entry route for a degree course is via an Art and Design Foundation diploma course (generally taken after A levels or equivalent); other entry routes include a relevant BTEC National qualification or a 12-unit A level in Applied Art and Design. Some degree courses are broad-based; others are more specialised. Some courses have a strong business or manufacturing emphasis. Foundation degrees offer an alternative route through higher education; they can be taken on a full- or part-time basis.

Designing rooms would be fun.

4. Part-time courses, such as those leading to ABC awards, are offered in areas of the country where the clothing industry is strong and are relevant for those already in employment.

5. Once you get into the industry you may be working from the bottom up, learning many skills on the job in the cutting room with the cutters and machinists.

How about designing costumes like this?

Want to make hats?

Opportunities for fashion designers

If you are interested in fashion, there are a variety of jobs that could be for you.

- tailor — sewing clothes for individuals
- textile designer — creating ideas and designs for textiles
- fashion marketer or merchandiser — working on the business side of fashion
- milliner — designing and making hats
- shoe designer and maker
- Embroidery - machine embroidery is widely used. Most design is done by people who have taken specialist courses.
- Theatrical costume designer and maker – for stage and TV - is a combination of design, dressmaking and historical research. It is a highly competitive field. Courses are available at a few art colleges and drama schools.
- industrial designer — creating and updating object designs, for example, toasters, toys or furniture
- interior designer — designing the look, feel and themes of rooms instead of clothes

Other related careers to consider:

Besides designers, the fashion industry also employs people in:

- buying, marketing, promotion, fashion and general management.
- Fashion retail sales
- Fashion photography
- Textile and surface designer
- Designer craftspeople
- Modelling
- Interior design.

Glossary

apparel — general term for clothes

brand — the specific maker of something, for example, Adidas, Nike

buyer — person who buys ranges of clothes from designers to sell in their employer's shops

colour scheme — colours chosen to be used together for clothes, interior design etc.

concept — idea

costing — estimating how much a garment will cost to make

garment — a specific piece of clothing

grading — different sizes, for example small, medium, large

merchandise — goods to be sold

outsourcing — contracting an outside company to work on a specific job

production — the making of something

prototype — first trial model of something made to test and improve the design

range — a collection of fashion

storyboard — collection of pictures and colours to show a designer's ideas

style book — book that shows the designs in the range

textile — woven cloth or fabric

texture — way something feels when you touch it

trademark — name or symbol protected by law, which manufacturers use to brand their product, for example, Coca-Cola sign

trend forecast — prediction of what will be in next season; an informed guess

Useful contacts, books and websites

Skillfast-UK – the Sector Skills Council for fashion and textiles *www.skillfast-uk.org*

Can U Cut It? a helpline for advice on careers in the fashion industry
Tel: 0800 06 88 07 *www.canucutit.co.uk*

Working in Fashion & Clothing – published by **DCSF** formerly DfES
www.connexions-direct.com/wifashandcloth

The following website provides information on career opportunities in the arts, including fashion design: *www.yourcreativefuture.org*

Information about **Graduate Fashion Week** can be found on: *www.gfw.org.uk*

Index